Speaking Blessings Over a Child's Life: The B—Attitudes (The Beatitudes)

Includes a Workbook

By Tawain J. Smith

Copyright

Speaking Blessings Over a Child's Life: The B—Attitudes (The Beatitudes)

Scripture references are taken from the Bible. Paraphrased for clarity and understanding for children.

This work was created for educational and inspirational purposes.

Published in the United States of America

First Edition

Author: Tawain J. Smith

Illustrations by Tawain J. Smith
Cover design by Tawain J. Smith
ISBN: 979-8-9955267-4-2
Published by Pratt-Winn Legacy Publishing

ESV (English Standard Version®)

Note to Parents

Scriptures in this book are based on the Beatitudes (Matthew 5:3–12; Luke 6:20–23) from the English Standard Version (ESV) *Bible*. To help young children understand, the verses have been carefully paraphrased in language suitable for children. Parents are encouraged to read the full Scripture together with their children.

Dedication

To the little hearts learning to love, to forgive, and to choose what is right—may these words guide your steps and remind you that God is always close by, watching over you.

Tawain “CC” Pratt

What Does Blessed Mean?

God's Way in the Bible

Being blessed means not just being happy, but having a deep joy and kindness on the inside that comes from God, not based on what is going on, but on the right relationship with Him.

You are special to God.

You are loved by God and walking in His way—no matter what is happening around you.

Introduction

Jesus taught us beautiful ways to live. He showed us how to be kind, how to love others, and how to choose what is right. *These special teachings are called the Beatitudes.* In this book, you will learn how to live these beautiful ways every day. And as you do… You will be walking in the "B—Attitudes" of Jesus.

You are deeply loved by God.

Jesus is not just describing feelings—He is showing us who we are in God's kingdom.

In God's kingdom, you are seen, loved, and held by Him.

You are His beautiful child.

Here are the special blessings from Jesus that show us how to have a heart like His.

The Poor in Spirit

The Poor in Spirit

"Blessed are those who know they need God."

(Matthew 5:3)

They are Part of God's Kingdom

"God's kingdom belongs to them."

Those Who Mourn

Those Who Mourn

"Blessed are those who feel sad."

(Matthew 5:4)

God Does not Leave Them Alone

"For God will make them feel better."

The Meek (Gentle)

The Meek (Gentle)

"Blessed are the gentle and kind."

(Matthew 5:5)

God Will Give Them What is Good

"For they will enjoy the good things God has made."

Those who Hunger and Thirst for Righteousness

Those who Hunger and Thirst for Righteousness

"Blessed are those who want to do what is right."

(Matthew 5:6)

God Will Fill Them with What is Good

"For God will make their hearts full and happy."

The Merciful

The Merciful

"Blessed are those who show mercy and forgive."

(Matthew 5:7)

God Will Forgive Them

"For God will be kind to them."

The Pure in Heart

The Pure in Heart

"Blessed are those whose hearts are clean."

(Matthew 5:8)

They Will Know God is Real

"For they shall see God."

The Peacemakers

The Peacemakers

"Blessed are those who help make peace."

(Matthew 5:9)

The Sons of God

"For they shall be called the children of God."

Those who are Treated Badly for Righteousness

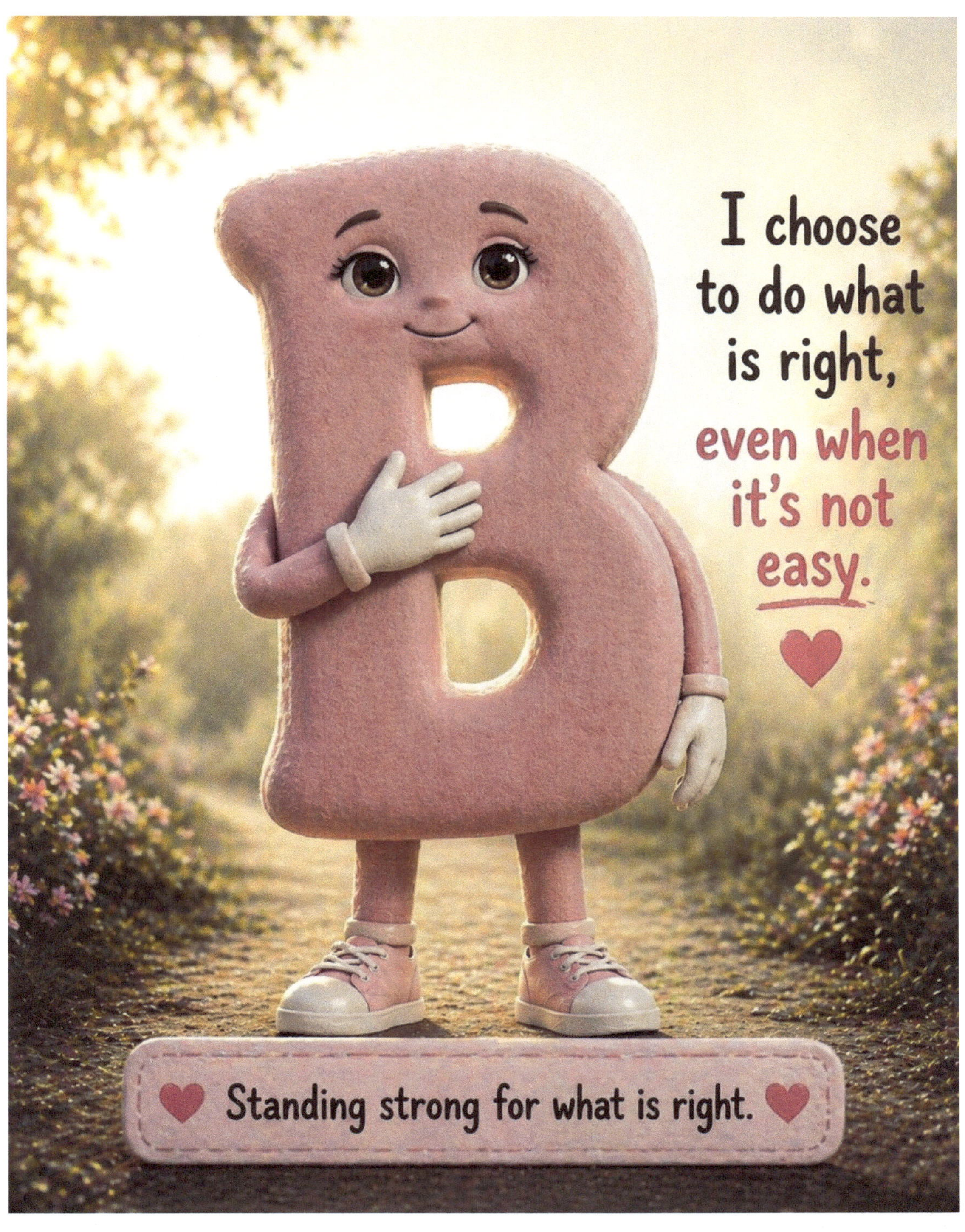

Those who are Treated Badly for Righteousness

"Blessed are those who are treated badly for doing what is right."

(Matthew 5:10)

They Belong to God

"For theirs is the kingdom of heaven," where He rules with love.

You who are Picked *On* and Lied *On*

You who are Picked *On* and Lied *On*

"Blessed are you when others say mean things about you and lie on you because you love Jesus."

(Matthew 5:11)

Celebrate and be Happy

Celebrate and be Happy

"When things are hard, be happy because God is with you."

(Matthew 5:12)

You are not Alone

"There were good people a long time ago who went through the same thing."

A Reward or Prize

Sometimes a reward is not a toy, a sticker, a hug, or someone saying, "Good job." Sometimes a reward is a happy feeling inside, or knowing God is proud of you, even if no one else sees.

What is one way you can be kind, gentle, or loving today?

Write and Draw Below This Line

Word Search

Find: MEEK • MERCY • PEACE • PURE • KIND •
LOVE

H	F	H	P	I	Y	C	R	J	A
P	J	K	S	C	W	J	Y	Q	G
E	N	E	R	N	T	J	N	O	F
A	H	E	J	I	Z	B	C	E	B
C	M	M	P	K	I	N	D	V	O
E	U	I	U	Q	R	U	P	O	W
K	E	V	R	G	C	N	G	L	U
U	O	I	E	F	L	N	X	S	K
U	R	G	K	D	B	W	H	I	Y
S	T	H	D	K	F	J	O	A	B

Matthew 5: 3–12 shows who *you are* in God's heart.

AND

Luke 6:20–23 shows how God meets you in *real life*.

These are ways God blesses us in everyday life—

even when things are not easy.

You Who are Poor

"When you do not have much, you can still trust God—He is with you."

(Luke 6:20)

You who are Hungry now—**God will Provide**

"When you feel empty or in need, God will take care of you."

(Luke 6:21)

You who are Sad / Weeping now (Joy is Coming)

"When you feel sad, God sees you—and joy will come."

You who are Left Out / Treated Badly

"When people are unkind because you follow Jesus,

you are still blessed."

(Luke 6:22)

The Answer

Be happy and celebrate—God sees you and has something special for you!"

(Luke 6:23)

What can you do when you feel sad, left out, or treated unkindly?

Write and Draw Below This Line

Word Search

Find: TRUST • SAD • JOY • BLESSED • JESUS • CARE

C	A	R	E	G	H	O	N	P	S
B	H	N	O	H	U	N	G	P	U
G	B	B	I	I	H	Q	G	Y	S
H	N	I	E	K	B	K	J	S	E
D	S	M	U	U	Z	O	W	X	J
T	R	U	S	T	Y	B	P	M	C
N	G	S	D	E	S	S	E	L	B
F	K	J	V	P	Z	U	K	N	Q
G	U	Z	V	Z	I	K	S	A	D
M	P	C	I	U	V	G	B	M	T

Closing Thought

God's ways are kind, gentle, and full of love. Each time you choose them, you are growing into who God made you to be.

You are living a blessed life when you follow Jesus.

Blessed are those who follow Jesus. As you live His ways, you are learning the Beatitudes—and living in the B—Attitudes of Jesus.

About the Author

Tawain J. Smith, lovingly known as "CC," was born on September 4, 1974. She began her life as Tawain Jeanette Pratt and, through the journey of marriage and motherhood, embraced the names Mrs. Tawain J. Winn and later Mrs. Tawain J. Smith. She is the devoted mother of two sons, Solomon P. Winn III and Jaylin P. Winn, and a loving mother by marriage to Stanton L. Smith II, all of whom she has raised and embraced with love, faith, and purpose.

With a deep passion for knowing God, Tawain is committed to sharing His truth in ways that are clear, meaningful, and accessible—especially for children. Her love for Scripture shapes how she teaches, nurtures, and encourages others in their walk of faith.

Some of the images in this book are inspired by her childhood and her sons' childhoods—memories that reflect love, growth, and God's faithfulness through every season.

As a child of God, Tawain believes that building a legacy is one of life's greatest callings. She sees legacy not only in what we leave behind, but in what we faithfully pass on—truth lived out, wisdom shared, and a life devoted to God.

Through *B–Attitudes*, she hopes to help children see God clearly, know Him personally, and carry His truth in their hearts for generations to come.

"Pratt" is her origin.

"Winn" is her journey.

"Legacy" is her purpose.

Tawain "CC" Pratt

A Son, A Blessing, A Bond

To my son by marriage,
Stanton L. Smith II—our beloved "Jr."

Though life brought us together in its own time,
love made room for something real and lasting.
Watching you grow into the man you are today
has been a quiet blessing—one marked by strength,
resilience, and a heart that continues to unfold.

From your days on the wrestling mat in high school,
where discipline and determination took root,
to your military service, where courage and commitment
were lived out with honor—your life tells a story
of perseverance and purpose.
Even now, as your career takes you across places and paths,
you carry that same strength and steadiness with you.

You may not have come from me,
but you are deeply cherished by me.
Your place in this family is not by chance—
it is by purpose, by grace, and by love.

I honor the man you have become
and the journey still ahead of you.
May you always walk in truth,
stand firm in who you are,
and never forget how deeply you are valued.

With love always,
Mom 💜

“Blessed are…”

These powerful words from Jesus have guided hearts for generations.

In this beautiful written children’s book, young readers are introduced to the timeless teachings of Jesus through simple words and meaningful lessons they can understand.

Inspired by the Beatitudes from the *Bible*, each page gently guides children to choose kindness, show love, and walk in God’s way—no matter what is happening around them.

Because being blessed is not about having everything… it is about knowing God, and knowing God is with you.

“Blessed” are the kind.

“Blessed” are the gentle.

“Blessed” are those who love God.

www.ingramcontent.com/pod-product-compliance
Lightning Source LLC
LaVergne TN
LVHW070150110826
845147LV00002B/367
* 9 7 9 8 9 9 5 5 2 6 7 4 2 *